More About What It Means

TO

Be Southern

More Perspectives
From a Girl Raised Southern

~

by Cecilia Budd Grimes

*More About
What It Means*

TO

Be Southern

Published by
Abram & vanWyck Publishers
North Carolina
www.EtiquetteMatters.com

Manufactured in U.S.A.

Design by Paula Chance, Atlanta, GA

Library of Congress Control Number 2002095033
ISBN 0-9708396-1-8
First Edition

WHEN I FIRST STARTED GIVING MY LITTLE PROGRAM, *What It Means To Be Southern,* I'd dress up the tables at ladies luncheons with little computer-generated cards listing things uniquely Southern: funny little expressions that pour from the mouths of Southerners, foods distinctive to the South, and a list of famous and accomplished people like Billy Graham and Oprah Winfrey and Patrick Swayze and Michael Jordan, who had grown up Southern. Inevitably, the ladies would come and ask if they could take one of the cards to show a friend or share with a relative. It seemed the book was asking to be born, but it wasn't until Brenda Pollard entered my life that the book became a reality. She asked me to speak at a ladies luncheon for the North Carolina Museum of History Associates at the Washington Duke Inn in Durham, and she gleefully added, *"We'll have a book signing to follow!"* The Lord sends us people we need in our lives, when we need them, and I'm grateful He sent Brenda Pollard my way. Bless your heart, Brenda, you're precious, lovely, and darlin'!

~

The person who took what I had envisioned in my head and created the look and layout of my Southern books is Paula Chance who, fortunately for our collaboration, was raised in Mississippi. When the first volume appeared, with my little sister and me on the front cover, I became distressed at the choice of that particular picture. My sister had died suddenly of a heart attack just the year before, and I had incorrectly thought it might be difficult for my mama to see the two of us on the cover of my book. Paula explained that rather than looking at it like that, I should realize that we were two little girls dressed to play, and that only a little Southern girl would be carrying along a pocketbook for such an occasion. Bless your heart, Paula, you were right, and Mama was fine with it, even pleased with the cover.

~

TABLE OF CONTENTS

SOME OF THE OLDER GENTLEMEN IN OUR LITTLE TOWN still answer the telephone with *"All Right."* They're the same folks that trade at the filling station, help their wives wash the window lights, sop gravy with their biscuits, and water their turnip greens with a hose pipe.

~1~

Southern ladies just love to go to the beauty parlor, and not just to get their hair done. It's said that you can hear news at the beauty shop that you don't hear anywhere else. You may hear news over the produce counter at the grocery store, as you're gathering your collard greens, and you may hear news at the garden club, as you're being reminded to cut your roses right above a five-leaf branch where a new bloom is set, or you may hear the news over the phone while you're resting in bed "stoved-up" (under the weather with a cold), but by then, it's probably old news. If you want to hear it first, you'd best go to the beauty parlor.

"Who are Your People?"

And Other Way of Connecting

WHEN SOUTHERNERS ASK, *"Who are your people?"* they are certainly not trying to be nosy. They're taught better than that, and certainly to mind their manners. What they are trying to establish is some common ground on which to have a pleasant conversation. Who do you know that they know? It's really a frame of reference, and certainly not a background check.

That's also true of the question, *"Where are you from?"* That's an inquiry into where you were born which is not necessarily where you live now. We're interested in knowing where you grew up, because we might know somebody you know, and then we can get on with that pleasant conversation we wanted to have in the first place. It certainly might introduce the subject of your homeplace, which is a very big topic of interest with Southerners.

Your homeplace is an important part of your

heritage in the South. That's where your people originated and where your extended family comes to gather for family reunions. It's the house where all the family memories were created and where your neighbors, or home folks, had their places a little piece down the road. And as you might imagine, your homeplace is where home folks are always welcome, *"itn't it?"*

Another question Southerners pose is *"Now tell me, where do you go to church?"* Southerners are also interested in where you attend church, so that's another question that's always forthcoming. Church affiliation is a big deal. You'll know it, too, in other ways, when you hear your Southern friends respond to a disconcerting remark with, *"Well, Lord, have mercy!"* I have one friend who says, *"Mercy me!"* when she's in distress. That's just an abbreviated version of the same idea.

~4~

Southerners connect with their neighbors.

Mama and Daddy had the same neighbors, the Spences, just about all their married life. Miss Anne and Mr. James had a little hill in front of their house where we played King on the Mountain. When the Spences decided to build across town, they saved the lot next door for Mama and Daddy so they could keep on being neighbors for a few more decades. Mama had her house plans ready right away. That way their children and grandchildren could grow up together. Four generations later, their great-grandchildren still find time to play together in our little town.

Pearls, Porches,

Pudding ...

Things Dear to Our Hearts

IT'S ONLY A MATTER OF TIME until a Southern lady is going to need pearls. That's not to say a lady must wait until she marries to get her precious pearls. Often your grandmother or your mama will lend you a string to wear on worthy occasions: like your piano recitals, family weddings, or to church on Sunday.

Real pearls aren't hard to distinguish. Besides their lovely luster, real pearls have a gritty feel when they are rubbed against other real pearls. That's because the basis of a real pearl is a granule of sand around which a pearly substance has been secreted by an oyster. Fake pearls are shiny man-made white and feel perfectly smooth when rubbed against other fake pearls. We don't learn this difference from the jewelers either; our women folk pass this important information to us early on.

One of the nice things about pearls is that you can wear them anywhere and with any outfit. It's been said that your smile on occasion may be fake, and nowadays sometimes your fingernails, but your pearls and your silver must be real.

~

Porches are for fine visitin'.

In large cities in other places, most people wouldn't drop by unannounced and certainly not uninvited. But in small towns throughout the South, it's considered a fine courtesy to drop by (Southerners drop by rather than drop in), rock on the porch, set a spell, and sip some sweet tea. Rather than regard that as intrusive, Southerners perceive it as neighborly. That's how they catch up on what's going on around town and stay interested in things.

Porches are just divine, and Southerners just love to while away the hours, rocking and watching the world go by. It's a shame there aren't as many porches as there used to be, due, we're told, to air-conditioning and people heading inside for where it's cool, because that's where a lot of old-time fine visiting went on.

As small children, we could be enticed away from the porch to go catch lightning bugs, which we gently placed in big Mason jars covered with lids poked with a few small holes. Sometimes we'd line the jars up on the porch steps and run play Kick the Can or Hide and Seek. Our parents continued to watch from the porch to be sure we played pretty. We were reminded *"Pretty is as pretty does,"* so much you'd have thought it was a refrain in the Cokesbury hymnals.

If the time gets away from you and you need to leave the visiting, you'll likely hear a send-off like, *"Come back, you hear."*

One of my Virginia friends was telling me about a lady who grew up in another part of the country. This lady walked over to her new neighbor's house to return a cake plate. After a nice chat, the lady got up to leave. As she was walking away, the Southern neighbor, in the spirit of true Southern hospitality, called out to her new friend, *"Come back, you hear!"* Unfamiliar with this customary remark made upon departure, the lady turned back around and immediately came back into the house. She thought she had left something behind.

Pretty Incredible Persimmon Pudding

Miss Evelyn is our little town's persimmon lady. She has persimmon trees along the road that leads into the front of her house, and most years she has a "gracious plenty" to share. She takes the persimmons that fall from the trees, removes the flat slither seeds from each pod, and presses the pulp through a sieve.

She then freezes the prepared pulp in one-pint square plastic containers. After they are set, she removes the portions from the freezer containers, wraps each in wax paper, and brings the persimmon pulp blocks by to Mama. Mama can re-wrap them in tin foil if she plans to keep them awhile. They go right in her freezer locker for later feasts.

Miss Evelyn's best reminder is never leave out the baking soda when we make our persimmon pudding. She says that's what keeps the pucker taste out. She says that people who don't like to eat persimmon pudding just haven't had the privilege of eating good persimmon pudding.

Authority that she is on all things persimmon, Miss Evelyn shared with me the old Southern belief that persimmons can forecast the weather. About September when the persimmon starts to ripen, she takes a sharp knife and slices a narrow flat persimmon seed down the middle to observe the inner white pattern. If the pattern appears to be a knife — long, linear, and pointed, that's a sign that there will be a winter of ice to cut. If the pattern has the appearance of a spoon, then shoveling snow in the coming winter will be the task. And if the pattern has the look of a fork, with stringy looking tines, we'll be eating greens.

Persimmon pudding at our house doesn't last long because our children would even eat it with breakfast, especially the buttery side pieces. Miss Evelyn says the way to make my boys happy is to cook the persimmon pudding in long, narrow aluminum ice trays so there'll be more buttery sides. Mama would leave her persimmon pudding out on the counter to cool and Daddy would cut an inch wedge all the way around the edges. You might say he ate it from the outside in.

Miss Evelyn's

PERSIMMON PUDDING

2 cups prepared persimmon pulp, thawed
2 large eggs
1 cup milk
1 cup sugar
3 tablespoons butter (not margarine)
1-1/2 cup plain flour, sifted
1/2 teaspoon salt
1/2 teaspoon baking soda
1/2 t teaspoon cinnamon
1/2 teaspoon nutmeg

Heat the oven to 325°.

Place the butter into a 13"x9" baking dish and
put immediately into the oven to melt while you
combine all the ingredients of the pudding.

Pour the batter directly into the
hot buttered pan, and bake until set,
between 45 minutes and an hour.

Serve hot or cold.
Store the pudding in the icebox.

Hissie Fits

A N D

Conniptions

And Other Southern Ways

SOUTHERN LADIES HAVE BEEN KNOWN to express their dismay, even their downright disgust with highly dramatic protestations., hissie fits and the like.

A hissie fit is a stomping up and down, arms-waving loud kind of highly agitated display. This is not to be confused with a "conniption" which is more like a take-your-breath-away reaction to something you've heard. Hissie fits are more prevalent than conniptions. Often conniptions just threaten to occur, but actually don't materialize, as in *"I just about had a conniption when she told me she was calling off the wedding and returning all the gifts."*

Southern gentlemen don't have hissie fits or conniptions, even though they're mighty familiar with them. They sometimes get in the middle of 'em and just watch 'em when they happen. When they become angry, they're *"fit to be tied."*

Southerners like to give you word pictures

when they describe goings-on — straight forward analogies that tune in the listener.

"*Getting too big for his britches*" would describe someone who was acting too proud or boasting too much. Britches and drawers are about the same thing. Granddaddy is gone now, but there's no telling how many times he would have been telling somebody to "*Pull up your drawers,*" with fashion trends being what they are these days.

Getting ready for bed would bring on a remark like, "*It's time to hit the hay.*" That's where you get your beauty sleep.

We understand "*drunk as skunk*" and "*high as a kite*" when someone's drinking gets out of hand.

You'll hear Southerners say:

> *Blind as a . . . bat*
> *Stiff as a . . . board*
> *Fat as a . . . tub of lard*
> *Bright as a . . . new penny*

Rough as a . . . cob
Smooth as . . . silk
Mean as a . . . snake

Other expressions Southerners use:

"That makes me so ill."

This remark has nothing to do with being sick.
It's just a Southerner's way of confirming that something someone said or did just didn't set well. It's
more like ill-tempered than ill feeling.

"Gimme some sugar."

Grandparents used to always greet us little ones
with this little remark. It had nothing to do with
needing more sugar for their sweet tea. They wanted
us *"to love their necks."* And we surely would. We'd
climb up on their laps and greet them with some
sweet kisses.

"might could"

This pair of verbs signals a hesitancy of sorts by Southerners. It means maybe, even possibly, but a definite commitment it is not.

"clean forgot"

Everybody everywhere has occasional lapses of memory. Southerners use this expression to be straightforward about things they've let slip their minds. *"I clean forgot to carry her to the grocery store. She was needin' some loaf bread."*

"right smart"

This reference is to an amount of something and not necessarily to somebody's IQ. *"We had right smart of rain last night, thank goodness!"*

"Shoot fire!"

This expression signals exasperation. *"You mean there's no more? Shoot fire! I was hoping to get another*

piece of Mary Frances's Brownstone cake. How about
Listeen Brown's coconut cake? Could I finagle a piece
of that?"

In the South, needing rain is often a hot
topic of conversation. With the drought we've
been having, you'll likely hear various petitions
for rain. *"What we need this summer is a real 'gully
washer.'"* Farmers could go from *"fair to middlin"* to
"plumb excited." That's the way we'd all feel if we
could just *"get shed of"* this terrible dry spell.

Southerners endure a lot of grief over our use
of "over yonder." Yonder is used all through the Bible,
so we don't understand why it's such a difficult
concept to grasp. It's the opposite of "right here."
It means "over there," and we'll gladly point y'all in
the general direction if you look perplexed about
locating it.

Sweet Tea Comes That Way . . .

It's not an add-to kind of thing.

SOUTHERNERS BRISTLE when they have to sweeten their own tea. It's not that they can't, or don't know how, it's just that everyone knows you can't sweeten tea properly when it's already had the ice added.

Sweet tea is our beverage of choice. Sweet tea comes already sweetened. It's not an add-to kind of thing.

It's nicely brewed tea to which sugar has already been added before it's poured over ice. It's a procedural thing with Southerners. Sweet tea is made as sweet tea from the beginning. That's a very big distinction.

"Sweet milk" is a term that confounds some people, too, even though it's just what we call regular whole milk, so as to make the distinction that we're not talking about buttermilk. Everybody knows that chocolate cakes taste so much better if they've been made with buttermilk.

If you read the history of carbonated beverages,

you'll learn that the South introduced soft drinks to the whole wide world. 7-Up™ and Dr. Pepper™ originated in Texas, Pepsi-Cola™ in New Bern, North Carolina, and Coca-Cola™ was created in Atlanta. Growing up, we had Nehi Orange, too. When I grew up, we always said "soft drinks"— never "soda" or "pop." A hard drink would be something with liquor added, like Bourbon and Branch (that's a term for water and an acknowledgment of the source from which it came) and almost but not quite like a Mint Julep, which sounds pretty benign, but actually has a wallop of whiskey added to the crushed ice, sugar water, and fresh mint sprigs.

Give a Southerner a small bottle of Coca-Cola™ and a pack of those salted peanuts and you'll see a Southern ritual played out right before your eyes. The peanuts are poured directly into the coke's glass bottle and because of the high salt content, the soft drink will begin to bubble. Lots of people might wonder what's next, but that's easy. A Southerner will "take a swig" of the concoction. In fact, that's been called a Southern lady's mixed drink.

"Nabs" (probably a shortened reference to Nabisco) is another popular accompaniment to soft drinks. If you have Nabs with your soft drink, don't request cheese crackers in the South, or you'll find yourself confronted with a plate full of saltine crackers with slices of cheese.

Not more than ten miles from our house, there's a little produce stand and woodyard by the highway. It sells all kinds of unusual things you'd likely not find most anywhere else: moonshine jelly, country ham side meat, molasses, sour wood honey, cold cokes in glass bottles and packs of peanuts to go with them, and lots of Elvis pictures and clocks. They do a brisk business.

Sweet Tea, Made Real

Fill a small pot with 4 cups of water and bring to a boil. Immediately remove from the heat and place one large family-size tea bag (or 4 small teabags) into the steaming water. (The water will lose oxygen as it boils, so it is important to the flavor to remove the water from the heat as quickly as the bubbling appears.)

Steep the tea for 5 minutes, no longer. Fill a large pitcher with 7 cups of cold water and add one heaping cup of sugar. Pour the steeped warm tea into the cold water and stir. Serve over ice. Add lemon, if desired.

"Y'all Better . . ."

Some More Rules We're Taught to Follow

Never wash your iron frying pans with a lot of soap and water.

You're just supposed to rinse 'em out and wipe 'em with Crisco before you put 'em up.

Only professional cooks could justify this many, but I've got five large iron frying pans, all with some age on them. One I got when I married, two are my grandmothers' and the other two came from my husband's grandmothers. I've got a small one, too, that I use to toast pimento cheese sandwiches. These skillets are important things to pass down, especially if you like to cook fried green tomatoes or Pineapple Upside-Down Cake. The ones that have pouring lips on the side are real handy for pouring up your bacon grease.

There's no tellin' how many pounds of bacon have been fried among those five frying pans, or how much tomato gravy's been stirred.

Granny Thomas's

FRIED GREEN TOMATOES

3-4 green* tomatoes
cornmeal
salt to taste
shortening, usually lard
with a little bacon grease added for flavor

Cut the tomatoes into slices about 1/4" thick.

Melt the shortening in a heavy iron skillet.
Combine the salt and the cornmeal.

After dredging the tomatoes in cornmeal,
gently drop them into the hot shortening.

Fry on medium high. After browning
on both sides, remove from the heat,
and immediately drain on paper towels.

*Granny would also use yellow tomatoes, and
even pink tomatoes that were just beginning to
ripen. A proper frying tomato must not be fully
ripe or it will melt to mush when put into the
hot shortening.

Be tactful and sensitive to the perceptions of others.

Choose your words carefully so as not to offend.

We simply don't like people *"to cut their eyes at us"* because we know it's usually done to convey displeasure. Sometimes we'd just rather they *"made out like"* everything was *"right as rain."* That way we wouldn't have our Southern sensibilities offended.

Likewise, we wouldn't want to offer offense ourselves. That's why when a genuine compliment can't be forthcoming, a Southerner will resort to ambiguous adjectives like "interesting" or "unbelievable." We might mean it one way, but it can easily be interpreted to mean another. In fact, it might sound complimentary, even if we didn't mean it that way.

"Tell me what you think about my suggestions for the new furniture in the church parlor."

"Interesting."

"What did you think about how she's decorated her house?"

"Interesting."

"Unbelievable" works the same way. It's nice because, like interesting, it doesn't sound harsh. Tone of voice is the give-away here.

"How was your new wife's first venture into cooking pork chops"?

"Unbelievable."

"How was your vacation with your in-laws?"

"It was unbelievable."

When a Southern gentleman is ready to depart a gathering, even when prevailed upon by the hosts to remain, he'll use a handy little exit remark like, "Well, I need to be going. I've got to get home and feed the dogs." No one could argue against that as a valid reason, and an important one, to be on his way, and no hostess would ever be offended.

Southerners religiously follow the "Bless your heart" rule.

If you've ever wondered if someone is Southern born or not, just listen to their conversation. You're bound to hear them sprinkle throughout the conversation, "Bless your heart," at least once or twice while they're talking. Southerners pronounce people blessed for lots of reasons — sometimes it's just the only appropriate remark to make. It's handy, too, when something less than kind is said, *"I noticed she's put on a little weight, Bless her heart."* or *"He just can't seem to understand that you don't wear a plaid tie with a patterned sports jacket, Bless his heart."*

And one rule all Southerners love — serve fruit cake at Christmastime. Here's Mama's version of fruit cake cookies:

Ruth Virginia's

FRUIT CAKE COOKIES

1 stick of butter

1-1/3 cups brown sugar

2 eggs

1 cup plain flour, unsifted

1 teaspoon vanilla

2 cups pecans, chopped

1/2 pound candied citron, chopped

1/2 pound candied cherries, red and green

6 slices of candied pineapple, cut up

(Grocery stores throughout the South stock these candied fruits during the Thanksgiving and Christmas seasons.)

To make the batter, cream together the butter and brown sugar. Add the eggs. Stir in the flour and add the vanilla.

Grease a 13"x9"x2" baking dish. Pour the chopped pecans into the dish. Spread the batter over the nuts. Lightly press the candied fruits into the batter. Bake for approximately 45 minutes at 300°.

Southern Children are "JUST PRECIOUS" Bless Their Hearts...

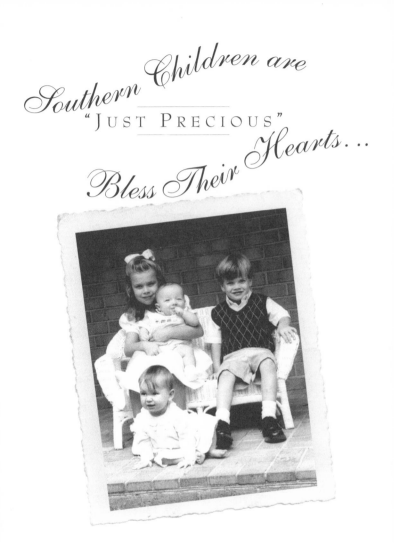

*Southern children
are taught Southern ways early on.*

SOUTHERNERS MAY SMILE when you compliment their children, but they always have an ear open for the appropriate adjectives.

"Your precious granddaughter was wearing a darlin' little dress at the piano recital, and she had such lovely manners at the reception."

Southerners prefer that their chidlren be described as *precious*, *lovely*, or *darlin'*, which are top-tier compli- ments, rather than nice, cute, or sweet, which, while true, are more ordinary ways of describing things, and to a Southerner's ear, less complimentary choices.

~

Patent leather falls under the A to A rule. You're taught to wear your shiny patent leather shoes from April to August, but after that they must be put away until another season.

My friend, Peggy McBrayer, shared a true story of her growing up years. One Easter, it snowed in her little town. She had new white shoes to wear, (as Southern ladies follow the rule that Easter Sunday morning is the first day of the season for wearing white shoes) and she had her heart set on wearing them. Her mother told her she would have to wear her black leather shoes one more Sunday, *"owing to the weather."* Miss Peggy cried and cried. Realizing her distress, her sweet daddy took her aside, started drying her tears, told her to stop crying and put on her black shoes like her mama said, but to carry her new white shoes to the car. When she got to church, he let her change into her new Easter shoes. Her daddy, like my daddy, always came to the rescue.

Often my daddy's mama would keep me at her house while my mama ran errands. Little girl that I was, I wanted to know when my mama and daddy would return. My grandmother's answer was

always the same, *"to-reckly."*
I came to understand that
was in a little while.

Daddy measured time
in a different way. He'd

take our black Gordon setter,
my beloved pet, Dobbin, out quail huntin'. When
we'd ask when he'd be back, his reply was always
"dark-thirty." He was hoping to bring back a mess
of quail (enough for a meal). We'd eat them with
biscuits for supper and hope we were lucky enough
to get the hoe cake.

Children of the South who'd be off to visit
their grandparents would be reminded of three
things. *"Don't forget to take your good manners, your
Sunday-go-to-meeting clothes, and your step-ins."* Good
manners meant that we were to say *"Yes Ma'm"* and
"No Sir," and *"thank you"* and *"please,"* without fail.

We were never to interrupt a grown-up and stand up, as a sign of respect, when an adult entered the room. Our Sunday clothes were dress-up and included things like little white gloves and matching white socks. And the step-ins, of course, were our underwear.

After our newest little grandson Tucker was born, three people in the same day remarked he was the "spittin' image" of his Great-Granddaddy. That's an old expression for "spirit and image," but Southerners have, over the years, just run the words together. It's sorta the same way "chess pie" got its name from "jest (just) pie."

Southerners just adore double names. Giving a child two names usually results in making more than one person happy when you're trying to honor family members. Our firstborn son was named for two of his grandfathers, and we still call him by his double name, John Thomas. My sister named her daughters Jennie Claire, for both of her grandmothers, and Alisa-Marie. (Her mother was an Elvis fan.) Most Southerners really know someone named Sue Ellen. There was a Sue Ellen rooming on my hall when I went to college, and that was a long time before Sue Ellen became such a prominent name on the television saga, *Dallas.* In my circle of friends, there's a Mary John, Mary Helen, Sarah Rebecca, Virginia Mae, Mary Frances, Barbara Anne, Effie Mae, and, of course, Mama. She's Ruth Virginia. More often than not, they are addressed by their double names. My husband has friends named Bubba, and Buddy, John Henry and Roy Marvin.

Dinner and Supper

AREN'T

the Same Thing

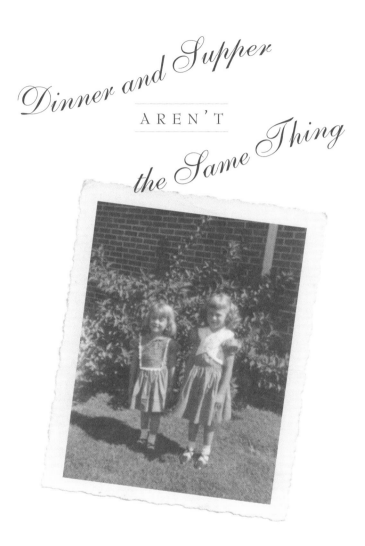

Sunday dinner is always right after church.

IN OUR LITTLE TOWN, Mrs. Huddleston, a 'widow woman' who excelled at Southern cooking, would serve Sunday dinner in her fine home on South Dogwood Avenue. Right after church, our family would head for Mrs. Huddleston's, but because there was usually a crowd, we'd wait our turn out on her wide white front porch. The swing to the left of the door was my favorite spot to wait.

Now this was a real Southern dinner we were served — right in the middle of the day and therefore not to be confused with supper. Sunday dinner was a glorious feast with snap beans, floating in 'pot liquor' (the good juices that the fatback produced during cooking), butterbeans and corn, fried apples, and homemade bread to accompany the country ham and fried chicken. There were always biscuits, too, with lots of homemade blackberry jelly.

Mrs. Huddleston had a wood-burning stove and

an electric stove, though I wasn't aware of it at the time, and I remember lovely cloth napkins and her tables always draped with crisply ironed white linens.

This fine lady was noted for putting a little bit of grated apple in her chicken salad. And, of course, being a proper Southern cook, she only used white meat in her chicken salad.

Mrs. Huddleston knew that Sunday dinner was the big meal of the day, and she fed almost everybody from church. After the caramel cake dessert, with inch-thick brown sugar icing, my sister and I would head back out to the swing on the porch to determine our fortune with the "pulley bone." It was our favorite piece of fried chicken, and we knew Mrs. Huddleston, like our mother, always cut up a chicken so there would be an extra piece of white meat.

Kate's Ice Cream Salad

2 cups sour cream
3/4 cup sugar
Juice of one whole lemon, at least 1/3 cup
1 small can of crushed pineapple,
somewhat drained
1/2 cup red or green (or both)
maraschino cherries
3/4 cup pecans, chopped
1 large banana, chopped in very small chunks

Combine all the ingredients,
stir well, and freeze.
Thaw slightly before serving.

When I make this recipe, I use a small
Tupperware™ container that has a removable
center disk at the bottom. When you release the
disk, the ice cream salad pops out neatly from
the sides and is ready for serving.

Devotion to

THE

Dearly Departed

Funeral Occasions and Tending Graves

SOUTHERNERS TAKE THEIR DEVOTION to the dearly departed quite seriously. Funerals are more than just services dedicated to those who have gone on to their rewards. Food is a big part of the goings-on, and complete meals provided by and shared with friends and neighbors abound. It is customary to invite the out-of-town visitors to lunch after the funeral service, and often these occasions are hosted in the fellowship halls of churches in the South. Food and funerals are just inseparable.

The ladies of the church bring their specialties: deviled eggs on proper deviled egg plates, platters of hot fried chicken, sweet potatoes topped with brown sugar and pecans, custard-based macaroni and cheese (not made from a box), fresh creamed corn, Jell-O™ salads made with pineapple and marshmallows, and yeast rolls with bowls of honey and homemade apple jellies and fig preserves. They lay it all out on long tables from which the bereaved family and their guests partake. The best cooks in the church always bring banana puddings. The ladies of the church who make up the benevolence committee serve the food and pour the sweet tea, too.

We were all sitting around a luncheon table, celebrating Becky Magruder's eighty-sixth birthday, when one of her friends, Miss Peggy, remarked, *"You know I've been tending thirteen graves all by myself, and I've been thinking of cutting back."*

"Thirteen!" we said, *"Heavenly days, that's a lot."* She explained that she was still tending her late husband's people's graves as well as her own family's. No doubt that's a lot of weeding and tending, and she reminded us we had no idea how many lilies that involved at Easter and how much holly and berries she had to tote at Christmas.

We know that people all over the world pay this kind of respect to their ancestors. It's just in the South we arrange big events around this tradition. Southerners often have many generations of family living and dying in the same community, and so they feel compelled to be attentive because they're close by and want to be properly respectful.

My college friend Becky who lives at the coast continues to carry on the tradition that her mother taught her about tending family graves. It's a family obligation, and so when Becky keeps her precious little grandson Gray on Tuesdays, she often packs him up, taking along a picnic lunch, and they go to tend the family plot right there on one of the raised corner plots of the old town cemetery. She's teaching him essentials, like she was taught, early on.

Whole church congregations pay respect and tend graves on occasions called Celebration Sundays, because the church folk realize how important it is to celebrate your people and honor their last resting places on this earth. They eat before, during, and after they celebrate.

You'll likely find old-fashion potato salad at such goings-on. There are usually two kinds served, one yellow-looking, which is mustard-based and another white, because it's mayonnaise-based — and served in big bowls, too, because there are lots to feed. There's probably a little mayonnaise in the yellow-looking potato salad and a little mustard in the white version. Mostly it's a matter of proportions.

At least 20-25 people can take a heaping serving from this potato salad. It's the white kind.

Mary Helen's

OLD-FASHION
POTATO SALAD

5 pounds. of white potatoes
6 large eggs, boiled
2/3 quart mayonnaise
2 tablespoons mustard
2 tablespoons celery seed
1 large onion, chopped
1/2 pint sweet pickle chips
2 cups celery, chopped
Salt and pepper to taste

Peel the potatoes, dice into small chunks
and boil in water until cooked.
(Select potatoes that are about the same size
so they'll cook evenly. Don't overcook.
Test with a fork to be sure the potatoes are cooked
but still hold together.) Drain potatoes.

Chop the hard-boiled eggs, and add to the
potatoes with all the remaining ingredients.
Mix well and chill for at least one hour.

Becky's

BANANA PUDDING

1-1/2 cup evaporated milk

1-1/2 cup water

4 eggs, separated

1 cup milk (She uses skim.)

2/3 cup flour

1-1/2 cup sugar

dash of salt

1 stick of butter

2 tablespoons vanilla extract

1 box (12 ounces) Nabisco Nilla™ wafers

2 bananas

1/2 teaspoon cream of tartar

8 tablespoons granulated sugar

~ Continued ~

BECKY'S BANANA PUDDING

~ Continued ~

~49~

Put the evaporated milk and water into a saucepan. Warm on the stove on low temperature while you mix the other ingredients. In a mixing bowl, combine the skim milk, flour, sugar, salt, and the yolks of the eggs. Set egg whites aside to use for meringue. (She uses an eggbeater.)

Add this mixture to the warmed milk in the saucepan. Over medium heat, cook slowly until the mixture thickens, stirring often to keep the mixture from sticking on the bottom of the saucepan. When the pudding has thickened, remove from the heat. Add the stick of butter and the vanilla extract. Leave pudding to cool to room temperature. (She puts hers in the refrigerator at this point and refrigerates overnight. She finishes the pudding the following morning.)*

When ready to assemble the pudding, prepare the meringue by beating the egg whites and

BECKY'S BANANA PUDDING

~ Continued ~

adding 1/2 teaspoon of cream of tartar. Slowly
add sugar, one tablespoon at the time, until
peaks form. Using the same beaters, combine
the stiff egg whites and the cool pudding.

Select an 8"x12" pan and cover the bottom
with a layer of vanilla wafers. Stand a few wafers
along the sides. (The wafers can be scattered,
sometimes two-deep in places.) Cover the
wafers with a layer of pudding. Add another
layer of wafers in a single layer. Slice bananas
thinly and cover the wafers. Add the remaining
pudding. Top with beaten meringue. Bake in a
400° oven until meringue browns, approximately 15 minutes. Serves 8.

*This recipe may be made in one day, but the
pudding must be cool in order to move to the
next step. If the pudding is put together while
it is hot, the heat cooks the bananas and they
turn dark.

Lookin' for Some Land

A N D

How to Find It

~

LOTS OF PEOPLE WANT THEIR OWN LAND. I remember Daddy saying that land is always a good investment because there's not going to be anymore.

There was a couple that came to our little community asking for some help in locating a piece of property right outside town. They were under the mistaken impression that the Emerson farm was on the market. It fell to me to explain the error of their ways.

"Now what you're asking to see is one of the finest pieces of land in the whole county. It's perched on that high hill where you can see to the Uwharrie mountain range and that's all the way to the next county. Let me tell you how to get there. You're going to love the view. Everybody does.

"Go right on out this same road, it's old 64, and keep on going past where Mr. Buckner's filling station used to be. You'll soon see the Emerson's picket fences.

Mr. Emerson made a point about not wanting any of those new vinyl fences you see everywhere — I mean they're all right, but they're not really real, if you know what I mean — and he even hired the FFA, that's the Future Farmers of America, club over at the high school to paint all those boards slap-white. He taught over there at the school before he went to work for Farm Credit, so that was nice. Turn left.

"There's no way for you to know this, but my grand-daddy on my mama's side actually built that house back when he first came to town. In fact, if you go down the back stairs — Mr. Emerson showed it to me one time — you'll see my granddaddy's name written on one of the boards going to the basement. And that front porch is just to die for — it's really a wide veranda, and there's a gracious plenty of room to walk around, even with all their nice white wicker rocking chairs. You can go in the front door from right there, or walk around the side and enter what used to be the front parlor — all from right there on that wide front porch.

You probably notice, too, that they have a little guest house on the side of the property. Every year our former preacher — he's retired now after thirty years at the same Baptist church, can you believe it? — comes with his wife to escape the Florida heat and visit relatives and old church friends. They enjoy Florida, because that's where their grandchildren are, but we all just get so excited having them here, talking about old times, and that guest house just makes it so easy and convenient and all. They stay about a whole month.

"The same barns are still there, painted red — wouldn't you know it? — and when we ride around on Sunday afternoons with Mama, she always wants to point out where all the different kinds of iris were planted near the porte-cochere and how many apple, peach, and cherry trees were in the orchard when she was a little girl living there. But it's the Emerson place now, and it's been in their family actually longer than it was in ours. Mama always comments that she's so proud somebody got her homeplace that keeps it up so nice.

"Head on up the hill, and the house and barns will come into sight. It's a pretty place, no doubt about it. I mean every Fourth of July they have a big barbecue and put the invitation right in the church bulletin, so everybody in the church will come and lots of out-of-town folks, too, and everybody comments on just what you've been told. It's a mighty pretty place.

"But the fact that you're inquiring about purchasing the Emerson place gives me pause. I know for a fact that besides all the history there, they still have one daughter who has her heart set on marrying there, and just last week they were telling me they have plans to establish a little family cemetery right there on the property, out back near the gazebo.

"All I can think is you must have been misinformed. It's never been on the market; I can't imagine that it would be. So even if your wife has her heart set on it, y'all best put it out of your minds. What I bet they were talking about when they told you there was a farm for sale with lots of pasture and a big white house is the old Edwards place. Y'all want me to show y'all how to get there?"

Growing up Southern is a privilege really,
just ask any born and bred Southerner.
That's why we keep on reminding our children
and our grandchildren that very thing.
We don't become Southern, we're born that way,
and we have a lot of precious people to thank for that.
Bless their hearts.